45 Minutes to Mastery

Malcolm Dewey

Copyright

Copyright © 2024 by Malcolm Dewey

Table of Contents

Introduction: The Problem and Solutions

Do you ever feel like your passion for painting is slipping through your fingers, lost amidst the demands of daily life, leaving you with too little time to work on your art? You're not alone. Many aspiring and experienced artists struggle to find the time to nurture their craft, feeling the weight of frustration and guilt when they can't dedicate hours to their easels. The reality of juggling commitments, work, and personal life often leaves little room for creative expression, and the dream of becoming a better painter feels increasingly out of reach.

Now, imagine a different scenario. What if you could make significant strides in your painting skills with just 45 minutes a day? This book promises to guide you in transforming those fleeting moments into powerful bursts of creativity. It's about making every minute count and seeing real progress without sacrificing your other responsibilities.

Inside these pages, you'll receive practical strategies tailored for artists that are short on time but big on ambition. Like you, of course. From quick, impactful exercises to efficient planning and mindset shifts, this book is your key to making every minute count. Whether you're a beginner looking to build foundational skills or an experienced painter seeking to refine your technique, this book offers a roadmap to consistent improvement, no matter how busy your schedule.

Join us on this journey to master the art of painting in short, productive sessions. Embrace the challenge of working within constraints, and watch as your skills flourish. Let's turn those 45 minutes a day into a powerful tool for artistic growth, ensuring that your passion for painting survives and thrives amidst everyday life's hustle and bustle.

Sounds good, right? I should know because this is how I built up my career as a full-time artist while juggling a thriving law practice, helping to homeschool my two boys, and still having time for a family life. It sounds insane, but it worked. Here I am today, living the life of a professional artist. If I can do it, so can anyone.

Let's go after it!

Best wishes

Malcolm

Small Paintings

As a beginner, the size of a canvas can often loom large in your mind. Many artists feel an unspoken pressure to create grand masterpieces, resulting in long hours spent laboring over details and often leaving them disheartened when they don't meet their expectations. Sound familiar? I have been there myself, and the results were not good. However, what if I told you that some of the most profound artistic growth occurs not from tackling vast canvases but rather through small, quick paintings completed in a single session? We also call this alla prima painting, which is a painting completed in one session.

The concept behind small paintings is deceptively simple yet profoundly impactful. By working on smaller pieces, artists can lower their stakes and create without being bogged down by completing so much territory. Trust me, a large painting needs a huge amount of information to be viable. However, a smaller work such as a 10x12 inch painting only needs a few large brushstrokes to describe a tree, for example. Each painting becomes an opportunity for exploration rather than a test of skill or endurance. This approach encourages daily practice—an essential component of improvement—allowing you to paint regularly without feeling overwhelmed by the enormity of larger works.

My mantra used to be a painting a day. I tried to keep up with that approach for at least three years. Of course, there were missed days, but not that many. It did not matter if the painting was on a panel, a canvas, or primed paper. I did the work, and that has paid me back tenfold. Daily painting doesn't mean dedicating your entire day to art; instead, it could involve setting aside just a short period each day to create something small. Picture this: you wake up in the morning with your coffee steaming beside you and decide to spend just 15 or 20 minutes on a tiny canvas. You may focus on capturing the delicate play of light over an apple or experimenting with colors as they blend into one another in a sunset sky. In this brief session, you're honing your skills and developing a habit that nurtures creativity. One effective method for harnessing this practice is through creating miniature series centered around common themes or subjects. Think about what inspires you—perhaps it's flowers blooming in your garden or unique shadows cast by everyday objects around your home. By producing several small works based on these themes, you'll begin to see trends emerge within your style while tracking progress over time. These mini-series can also serve as building blocks for more extensive projects down the line or simply stand alone as cohesive collections that showcase your evolution as an artist. For instance, if you've created five different interpretations of sunflowers in various positions and moods throughout changing lighting conditions, you've practiced and developed insights into how color and form interact at different times of the day.

Let's consider practical steps towards incorporating small paintings into your routine effectively: 1. **Set Aside Time**: Dedicate specific times when painting becomes non-negotiable—whether it's first thing in the morning before life gets hectic or during quiet moments after work. 2. **Gather Your Materials**: Keep supplies accessible; having paints ready helps eliminate excuses when it's time to paint! Consider having painting panels at hand so that whenever inspiration strikes—or even when it doesn't—you are prepared. Need lots of panels? No problem. You can get 3mm MDF panels cut in bulk at a timber merchant. I even did this over the phone and had the cut panels delivered by courier. The savings are enormous, and I have enough panels to paint for six months. 3. **Choose Your Subject**: Simplify decision-making by selecting subject matter ahead of time based on themes you're passionate about exploring further. Your photos are a good place to start. 4. **Embrace Mistakes**: Allow yourself permission to fail! Remember that every piece doesn't need to be completed in one sitting; sometimes, it's about capturing moments rather than achieving perfection right away. Other times, you are doing a basic blocking of a subject. That is enough if you run out of time or energy. You are learning to assess a subject and get the basic shapes in place. Never be discouraged by a result. Each work is the stepping stone to the next one. Improvement is not linear either. There are good days and bad days. 5. **Reflect Regularly**: After completing each piece (or series), evaluate what worked well and what could improve next time around. This reflection solidifies learning experiences while encouraging future endeavors. By consistently embracing these steps over weeks and months through daily practices focused on smaller artworks instead of large projects requiring extensive commitments upfront, you will undoubtedly make significant improvements—and perhaps even more importantly, a newfound sense of enjoyment throughout your creative journey! Ultimately, creating small paintings isn't just about finishing pieces quickly; it's cultivating an attitude where experimentation thrives alongside skill development at every turn while allowing space for joy within creativity itself! Much like fitness routines built upon consistency yield results, so too does regular painting, study, and creative endeavor help you rise to amazing levels of skill.

Assignment:

1. Set up your painting materials where you can start working at short notice;
2. Make a schedule. Set out the time of day you intend to paint. Inform any other family members that this is your work time. It is not long but a "do not disturb" time.
3. Consider a painting project. Perhaps a series of similar subjects? Or will it be a practical learning period, like teaching yourself how to mix colors?
4. Finally, try to record your progress in a bullet journal. Include a few entries confirming that you completed a session, what you did, and what you want to try the following day. Keeping a journal like this can be a significant help in tracking your development.

Focused Exercises

As artists, we often find ourselves grappling with the complexities of our craft. Whether you're a beginner or an experienced painter, there are moments when the canvas seems daunting and the tools unfamiliar. It's all you can do just get a few paint strokes on the canvas before you find yourself stuck. Pack it in because time is up, and it still looks like there is too much to learn. The key to overcoming this struggle lies in consistent practice, particularly through focused exercises that can help us hone our skills and build confidence. This chapter will explore effective warm-up exercises, delve into color-mixing techniques, and discuss how experimenting with brush strokes can elevate our work. **Warm Up Exercises:**

The significance of warm-up exercises cannot be overstated. Just as athletes take time to stretch and prepare their bodies before a game or performance, artists need to engage in activities that loosen up both their minds and hands before tackling a more involved piece. Quick sketches serve as an excellent way to get started. These sketches should not be about perfection; rather, they should focus on quickly capturing movement, form, or specific details. Set a five-minute timer and challenge yourself to prepare a small sketch or notan study within that timeframe. This exercise encourages spontaneity and helps you learn to make confident decisions under pressure.

What is a notan study? If you have not done so already, consider taking my free course on notans called *How to Add Power to Your Paintings*. In effect, these are value studies that reduce the scene to a number of major value shapes. It is the foundation for a strong painting. You could use black and white for a two-value study. A black marker pen and the white page will provide the values. You could add a middle value gray for another value. You could add a second lighter gray for a fourth value. Since most landscapes consist of four major values, you can see how this is a good start by establishing those big shapes from the start.

Instead of a marker you could use monochrome paint and create a painted value study. Mix ultramarine blue with burnt sienna and create a strong dark. Then add white to create your gray values. A monochrome value study is an excellent learning tool for assessing a landscape subject. This could take you a bit longer, but ten minutes should be plenty to do a value study or two. By working quickly, you train yourself to think and act more confidently.

The next step in the process is to do color value studies. Instead of a monochrome dark, you may now make it green, for example, and your light landscape yellow-green, your sky light blue, and so on. Try to get the colors to the correct value. Do studies like this for days or even weeks, and you will grow in skill and confidence. Painting becomes significantly easier when you can see and paint values on the canvas. In addition to quick sketches, practicing studies—whether they are still life or figure drawings—offers another benefit. A study allows you to analyze your subject closely without the pressure of it being a final piece. You might choose a single object from your surroundings—a vase or an apple—and dedicate your time to understanding its shape, light reflections, and textures through various angles and perspectives.

The goal is not just replication but deepening your observational skills. Learning to see like an artist. **Color Mixing:**

Color mixing is another foundational skill that every painter must develop over time. Understanding how colors interact is essential for creating depth in your paintings. Begin with simple exercises: take two primary colors—say red and yellow—and mix them in varying ratios on your palette until you achieve different shades of orange. Try using a warm red like cadmium red light. Then use a cool red like alizarin crimson. What do you observe about the richness of each mixture?

Use different yellows too. A cool yellow like lemon yellow and a warmer yellow like cadmium yellow deep. What happens when you mix a cool yellow with the reds. Now try the warm yellow with the reds. Compare the various orange colors to each other.

These different "shades" are distinguished by their relative color temperatures. In other words, compare one orange to another and decide which one looks warmer and cooler. This is how you train your eye to see color temperature by comparing one color to another.

The next step is to add white to your orange colors. A little white at a time and observe the changes. Note how the orange becomes lighter and cooler. You are altering the value and the color temperature. But don't stop there! Explore secondary colors by mixing blue with yellow for green or red with blue for purple; experiment further by incorporating white into these mixes as described above. Regularly engaging in dedicated color mixing practice—even for just five minutes—you'll develop an intuitive understanding of color relationships that will translate into pleasing results on the canvas. **Brushwork:**

Once you've warmed up through sketches and feel confident about color theory via mixing exercises, it's time to enhance your brushwork skills by experimenting with different strokes across small sections of canvas—or even on scrap paper if you prefer not to waste materials initially. Take note: each brush type offers unique possibilities—from stiff bristle brushes that create textured lines to softer brushes for smoother blending. Place a few paint piles on your palette and experiment with brushstrokes by varying the pressure. Also, note what happens with the speed of the stroke. The faster stroke produces a more energetic-looking result. Try short dabs versus long swipes; explore circular motions versus straight lines—the goal here is an exploration of brushwork technique using your brush and your arm. Hold your brush between your four fingers and the palm of your hand. The thumb lends support. Avoid holding the brush like it is a pencil. You are learning arm movements and wrist movements here. This makes for a more expressive stroke. Incorporating these focused exercises into your routine doesn't require much time; even dedicating fifteen minutes before diving into painting sessions can yield significant improvement over weeks as these practices build upon one another, cumulatively sharpening both technique mastery and creativity exploration! Ultimately, remember that artistic growth stems from patience alongside perseverance. Improve specific techniques one step at a time.

Assignment:

1) Study the notan sketch. Practice basic notan sketches first with marker pens, then with monochrome paint and then with color. Aim for correct values. 2) Color Mixing enriches comprehension of what makes up color: value and saturation. Practice mixes and adjusting color by adding white. 3) Brushstroke experimentation familiarizes you with various methods of communication through the brush. How you use brushwork will greatly determine your style of painting.

Structured Practice

Artists often find themselves in a cycle of inspiration and frustration. One moment, the urge to create surges through us; the next, we feel overwhelmed by the complexity of our craft. The key to breaking this cycle lies in structured practice—an approach that allows us to focus our efforts on specific skills and techniques without becoming bogged down by the enormity of our artistic aspirations. You have seen some of these ideas in the chapter on Focused Exercises. Structured practice involves setting clear intentions for each painting session and dedicating time to focused studies. This chapter will explore how timed studies can enhance your skills, why copying masters is a valuable exercise, and how both methods can lead you to becoming a more confident painter.

Incorporate these study methods into your daily routine at any stage of your career. Doing a few master studies, for example, can provide a welcome break for any jaded artist.

The Power of Timed Studies

Try setting aside just 15 or 20 minutes for an intense exploration of light or texture in your work. This method encourages you to concentrate deeply on one aspect without getting distracted by the larger composition. By using a timer, you create an urgent and liberating environment—the pressure allows for free expression while also pushing you to make decisions quickly. Start by selecting a subject—perhaps a simple still-life arrangement of a vase and flower or even an object from your surroundings. Place it under direct light, such as by a window, so that shadows play across its surface, providing ample opportunity for studying light and shadow. Once you've chosen your subject, set your timer for 15 minutes. As the timer begins, allow yourself to paint freely without overthinking every brushstroke. Focus solely on capturing light and shadow shapes: observe where highlights fall and where shadows deepen. In this short period, aim for boldness rather than perfection; let each stroke be intentional yet spontaneous, helping you develop confidence in your choices. Think of each stroke as a tile in a mosaic. It is okay if your final result looks like a series of distinct brushmarks placed side by side. Free yourself from the need, should you have it, to blend each stroke into the other stroke. Afterward, take some time to reflect on what worked well during those 15 minutes and what didn't resonate with you as much as you'd hoped. Did certain colors capture the essence better than others? Was there a brush technique that felt particularly effective? Use these reflections as stepping stones for future sessions—a way to build upon insights gained through structured practice.

Copying Masters: Learning Through Imitation

Another powerful method of structured practice is emulating established artists—those whose techniques have stood the test of time. Copying masters does not mean plagiarizing their work but engaging with it actively and thoughtfully as part of your learning process. You will see art students in museums doing exactly this while observing master paintings. If you are fortunate enough to have such museums in your city, then pay them a visit to study these works closely. Choose an artwork that inspires you—one whose color palette captivates you or whose brushwork seems effortless yet expressive. Set up your canvas alongside a printout or digital image of this masterpiece so that they exist side by side during your painting session. Now set another timer; this time, perhaps give yourself 20 minutes per section (such as sky versus foreground) depending on how complex the piece may be—but remember not to get too caught up in details initially! Focus first on matching colors accurately while mimicking their application style: observe whether they use soft blends or abrupt transitions between hues. I found copying Monet and Cezanne to be particularly helpful. Cezanne taught me an appreciation for dark value shapes in a landscape. With Monet, I learned how to create broken colors to depict water. Also, how to simply a figure in a landscape. Through copying these works stroke-by-stroke (or section-by-section), you'll begin developing an understanding of color mixing and composition choices made by experienced artists before us—a treasure trove waiting patiently within each painted canvas! Now please do not get caught up in creating an exact replica. This is not a forger's class. Rather you want to get color and values reasonably accurate. You will have your own brushwork characteristics. However, the likeness should be quite strong. Once again, when finished analyzing everything later during reflection moments afterward, it helps reinforce lessons learned along with practical application achieved throughout structured practices overall!

Assignment:

Pick out three artists whose works you admire and whose works you feel exemplify the style of painting you want to acquire. Set aside a week to paint these studies on a canvas about 25cm x 31cm. If it takes you longer, that is fine too. You could spend a week on one painting if you want to get the most out of it. Start by observing the composition. How has the artist laid out the painting? Where is the focal point? How has that been achieved? Then consider the light and shadow areas. Start by toning your canvas in a warm hue like burnt sienna. Then compose the scene. Then block in the major dark shapes and then middle value and light shapes. Then start refining with smaller shapes to capture the masterwork so that it is recognizable.

Preparation and Planning

An artist is often defined by the moments spent in front of the canvas, but a successful painting session begins long before the first brushstroke. Preparation and planning are essential components that can significantly enhance your work's quality while streamlining your creative process. In this chapter, we will explore how to gather materials effectively, plan your composition, and simplify your color choices so that you can maximize your painting time—ensuring that each 45-minute session brings you closer to achieving artistic growth. Gathering reference materials is one of the most important steps in preparing for a painting session. Reference images, whether photographs you've taken or artwork you have created that you want to rework, serve as vital tools for inspiration and accuracy. For this chapter, I will focus more on getting references from photographs as they are most convenient for short learning sessions. When selecting reference images, choosing ones that resonate with you emotionally or conceptually is best. This connection will not only make the process more enjoyable but will also infuse your work with authenticity. Getting photographs is not that difficult today since we have a phone camera. The trick is finding a subject and taking a good photograph.

By now, you have an idea about what makes a good composition. You have studied values and created notan paintings too. Look for light and shadow in a scene and your reference has a better chance of producing a good painting. If you love the scene, then all the better. As you collect these resources, consider creating a dedicated folder—either physical or digital—where all your references are stored together. Organizing these images based on themes or subject matter can make finding what you're looking for easier when it's time to paint. For example, if you focus on landscapes one week and portraits the next, separate folders allow quick access during preparation time.

What then? A practical consideration is how you use the reference when you want to paint. Do you print out the image? Do you work off your cellphone screen? Ideally, you should have your computer monitor close to your easel. Many artists use a tablet mounted next to their easel. The advantage of a screen is that the colors are accurate. The disadvantage is the potential costs. Another is the annoyance of the screen going into sleep mode, so you need to fiddle with settings. However, if you overcome these issues, then all is well. For me, the basic printout suffices. I can then get the composition worked out. Checking color information can be done on the desktop computer and planned out before I start painting. Whatever is practical for you at the moment is what you need to use. Do not waste time on obstacles. Once you've gathered your reference materials, it's time to plan your composition. A well-thought-out composition is the backbone of any successful painting; it dictates how elements interact within the frame and guide viewers' eyes through the piece. To create a strong composition without overwhelming yourself in detail during each session, sketch out several thumbnails before diving into a larger canvas piece. See the chapter on Focused Exercises. Thumbnails do not need to be intricate; they can be simple outlines capturing basic shapes and placements of objects within your artwork. This step allows you to experiment with various layouts quickly without committing too much time upfront. Once you've decided on a thumbnail sketch that speaks to you—the one where elements feel balanced—you can use this as a guide when working on your larger piece. A key aspect of planning includes determining which colors you'll use during each session. As artists often face an abundance of color options—a vast selection that can sometimes lead to decision fatigue—it's wise to adopt a limited color palette strategy for our 45-minute sessions. Limiting yourself doesn't mean sacrificing creativity; it encourages thoughtful exploration within specific constraints. Choosing three primary colors with white can provide enough variety while keeping things manageable as you work through different values and hues by mixing them directly on the palette. For instance, if you're working primarily with blue hues in one session—maybe ultramarine blue mixed with cadmium yellow—you'll find new greens while learning how to create warmer and cooler greens as you go. What colors to begin with? Use ultramarine blue, cadmium yellow lemon cadmium red light and titanium white.

Do you need any more colors? You can add more colors once you feel reasonably confident mixing secondary colors and the basic earth colors of burnt sienna and yellow ochre. In this case, consider adding cerulean blue (a cool blue), cadmium yellow deep (a warm yellow), and alizarin crimson (a cool red), plus burnt sienna and yellow ochre for convenience. With both reference materials organized and color palettes simplified into fewer choices than usual comes another crucial aspect: setting up an efficient workspace conducive to creativity! An uncluttered environment helps reduce distractions while keeping essential tools within arm's reach, which enhances flow during those focused bursts of painting activity. Before starting every new project—or even just moving into another painting day—take some time assessing what supplies are necessary: brushes (and sizes), canvases (or paper), palettes (for mixing), water containers (if using water-based mediums), rags or paper towels—all should be laid out neatly so they're readily accessible throughout those 45 minutes! Incorporating preparation into daily practice nurtures discipline alongside creativity—a crucial balance needed among artists seeking growth over perfectionism! Each step is taken prior—from gathering references through organizing the workspace will make the forty-five minutes count. Assignment:

Reference Materials: Gather references and plan your painting session for tomorrow. Set up a folder on your computer for digital image references into categories like seascapes, clouds, and so forth.

Limited Palette: Use a limited color palette to simplify your choices and speed up the painting process. Set out your paint tubes ready for your next session.

Composition

To follow up on Preparation and Planning, I would be remiss in not encouraging you to practice composition. Composition is crucial in landscape painting, as it guides the viewer's eye through the artwork and creates a harmonious and compelling scene. Here are some of the most important rules of composition in landscape painting:

1. Rule of Thirds

- A method to find the ideal point on the canvas to place your focal area. Divide your canvas into a 3x3 grid (like a tic-tac-toe board) and place your focal point at one of the four intersections.

- Application: Place key elements (e.g., the horizon, focal points) along these lines or at their intersections. This creates a balanced and engaging composition.

2. Leading Lines

- These are lines within the painting that guide the viewer's eye.

- Application: Use natural lines like rivers, paths, or utility poles to lead the viewer's gaze toward the focal point or through the painting. This adds depth and directs attention.

3. Focal Point

- The main area of interest in the painting. This is where the viewer's eye will be led. The hardest edges will also be used here.

- Application: Ensure a clear focal point, such as a tree, building, or mountain. This gives the viewer something to anchor their attention to. Avoid placing the focal point directly in the center; instead, use the rule of thirds.

4. Foreground, middle ground, and Background

- Dividing the landscape into three spatial planes.

- Application*: Create depth by including foreground, middle ground, and background elements. This helps to draw the viewer into the scene and provides a sense of scale and distance. Adjust your color, values, and brushwork to help suggest the recession of space into these areas. This is also known as aerial perspective.

5. Balance and Symmetry

- The distribution of visual weight within the composition.

- Application: Balance elements on either side of the painting to create harmony. This doesn't always mean symmetry; asymmetrical balance can be more dynamic and interesting and usually is. I prefer asymmetrical compositions.

6. Contrast and Color

- The use of differences in color, value, and texture.

- Application: Use contrast to highlight important areas and add interest. Color can guide the viewer's eye and evoke mood. For example, warm colors can advance and attract attention, while cool colors can recede. Avoid bright colors, strong value contrast, and eye-catching textures in places where you do not want the viewer to spend a lot of time looking. The picture edges and corners are examples of "stay-away" zones.

7. Simplification

- Reducing clutter and unnecessary details.

- Application: Focus on the essential elements and eliminate extraneous details. This helps to strengthen the composition and makes the painting more cohesive.

8. Framing

- Using elements within the painting to create a frame around the subject.

- Application: Use trees, archways, or other structures to frame the focal point. This directs the viewer's attention and adds depth.

9. Overlapping

- Placing one object in front of another.

- Application: Use overlapping elements to create a sense of depth and three-dimensionality. This technique helps to establish spatial relationships between objects. A row of overlapping trees, for instance, creates space. We associate overlapping shapes with a recession in the distance.

10. Repetition and Rhythm*

- The repeated use of shapes, lines, or colors.

- Application: Create visual rhythm by repeating elements throughout the painting. This adds unity and can lead the viewer's eye across the composition.

11. Negative Space

- The space around and between the subjects of an image.

- Application: Pay attention to the negative space to ensure it complements the positive elements. Well-used negative space can create balance and enhance the overall composition.

12. Vantage Point

- The perspective from which the scene is viewed.

- Application: Choose an interesting vantage point to add drama or interest. This could be a low viewpoint looking up or a high viewpoint looking down, depending on the effect you want to achieve.

Practical Tips:

- Thumbnail Sketches: Create small sketches to explore different compositions before starting the painting.

- Viewfinder: Use a viewfinder to isolate and focus on the best composition within your scene. For digital photos consider cropping the photo into the best composition.

- Feedback: Get feedback on your composition from peers or mentors to gain new perspectives and improve.

By considering these rules, you can create more dynamic, balanced, and visually appealing landscape paintings.

Mindset and Flexibility

Art is not just about the technique or the final product; it is also deeply rooted in the mindset we cultivate as artists. How we approach our creative endeavors can significantly affect our growth and enjoyment of painting. This chapter will explore the importance of setting realistic goals, recognizing small achievements, and being flexible within your artistic process. By fostering a positive mindset, you will improve your painting skills and enhance your overall experience as an artist. One of the first steps to developing a healthy artistic mindset is to set realistic goals. It is easy to fall into the trap of perfectionism or compare ourselves to established artists whose work we admire. This comparison can lead to frustration and discouragement if our progress does not align with the standards we set based on others' successes. Instead, focus on creating achievable objectives tailored to your current skill level and personal growth. Consider defining short-term goals for each painting session. For instance, rather than aiming to create a masterpiece in one sitting, challenge yourself with simpler targets, such as experimenting with a new color palette or mastering a specific brushstroke technique. These smaller tasks allow for manageable progress while reducing pressure and anxiety around performance. Celebrating small achievements becomes essential in reinforcing this positive mindset. Every time you complete a painting session—regardless of whether you consider it successful—acknowledge your effort and recognize what you've accomplished during that time frame. Perhaps you tried a new method that worked well or learned something valuable from an unsuccessful attempt; both are worthy accomplishments.

Taking time at the end of each session for reflection can help. Ask yourself what went well during your practice today. What did you learn about color mixing or composition? Did any unexpected discoveries arise while working? Documenting these reflections in an art journal can motivate you by allowing you to track your progress over time while showing how far you've come on this creative journey. Flexibility plays another crucial role in achieving sustained artistic growth. It often requires us to let go of rigid expectations surrounding our work's outcome or timeline. Embracing flexibility means understanding that creativity operates outside strict boundaries; sometimes, paintings will take longer than anticipated due to difficulties encountered along the way (such as lackluster inspiration). When faced with challenges like painter's block or frustrations tied directly back to perfectionism, the best remedy lies in accepting imperfection itself! Acknowledge when things do not turn out exactly as planned, instead shifting focus toward learning opportunities hidden within those 'mistakes.' Have no fear of judgment from external sources—including yourself! One of the biggest problems with many artists is an inherent fear of looking foolish. This goes back to traumatic school experiences, for example, and manifests in adult life when you give up because the work is not excellent. Stop that behavior, please. It hurts you more than you think. For example, If you're working on layers of colors but find that the colors intermix and become muddy, try stepping back to reevaluate what isn't working instead of throwing it all away in frustration. By remaining open-minded throughout every stage—from brainstorming concepts to final touches—you'll cultivate resilience against setbacks & discover innovative solutions previously overlooked. You will understand that pressure and perfectionism are merely self-imposed limitations not grounded in reality. Remember: Not every painting needs to be completed within one session! Giving yourself permission allows you to explore joyfully rather than obsessively honing in on single outcomes—a freeing realization that provides endless possibilities. So take heart; keep pushing forward daily—with patience and persistence.

As you develop these practices in nurturing both mindset & adaptability, remember to always return to core foundation principles in the previous chapters: 1) Creating small paintings regularly. 2) Engaging in focused exercises boosting skills gradually, 3) Structuring practice sessions towards mastery techniques, 4) Preparing thoughtfully before diving paintbrush hand, 5) Utilizing resources available online communities inspiring connection among peers willing to share experiences.

Utilize Resources

It is essential to recognize that you are not alone. The world is filled with resources designed to help you grow as an artist, providing tools, knowledge, and community support that can enhance your creative experience. This chapter will explore various resources available to artists at every level, focusing on online classes, social media platforms, and art communities. By utilizing these resources effectively, you can accelerate your learning and maintain motivation throughout your artistic journey. One of the most significant developments in recent years has been the rise of online learning platforms. There are many to choose from and you can find them by simply searching for these sites online. I need only add that I have my own online school platform. You can find links to that on my Painting Course page at malcolmdeweyfineart.com. The biggest challenge is not finding courses but actually completing the courses. Motivation is vital, and distractions are off the scale! That is why taking a course with someone who inspires you is important. Also, look for any community involvement so that you can share or at least see what others are getting up to with the school. Naturally, it helps to select a teacher working in a medium and style that appeals to you. A final tip is to follow a structured approach that actually teaches you the fundamentals of painting. I encourage artists to start with my course Learn to Paint with Impact as it sets out those basics that apply to all my subsequent painting classes. Without those fundamentals, beginners will always struggle with the more advanced painting classes. In addition to structured classes, YouTube has become an invaluable resource for artists seeking inspiration or guidance in their work. Many talented artists share their processes through tutorials, breaking down complex techniques into digestible steps. Whether it's a video demonstrating how to create texture using palette knives or tips for layering glazes effectively, YouTube offers endless content tailored to your specific interests. I, too, share a tremendous amount on YouTube, and this teaching and sharing has been very inspiring to me. The only caution with YouTube is that the lessons are not structured, so topics are scattered. Still, if you can get some basics behind you, you can find many excellent painting lessons to inspire your 45-minute painting sessions. Social media platforms also play a crucial role in connecting artists with valuable information and community support. Instagram is particularly popular among visual artists; many painters use this platform not only to showcase their work but also as a way to document their artistic process through stories or reels. Following other artists whose work resonates with you can provide both inspiration and insight into different approaches. Moreover, social media allows instant communication between creators around the globe; don't hesitate to engage by commenting on others' posts or asking questions about their techniques—many are more than willing to share insights from their creative journeys. The proviso is clear, however: social media can easily drain away your free time actually to paint. If you notice this happening, rather put your phone away and get to grips with actually painting. Most importantly—art communities often act as safe spaces where individuals feel comfortable sharing vulnerabilities associated with creating art: fears about failure; anxieties regarding comparisons made between themselves versus other successful figures seen elsewhere (both digitally & physically); doubts stemming from self-critique after completing pieces deemed less-than-stellar... The emotional support provided here cannot be understated! For this reason, I created a monthly live class on a membership model. The classes are smaller, but the members are committed to joining in and completing paintings. The critiques and community interaction are amazing, and I am very proud of the efforts put in by the members. This, to me, is far more rewarding than any social media interaction. This system is about doing, and action makes all the difference. Lastly, don't forget about books! There exist countless publications dedicated solely to improving painting skills, covering everything from foundational principles right up until advanced stylistic explorations showcasing renowned masters' works broken down step-by-step. These books allow readers to grasp the intricacies behind creating breathtaking imagery firsthand—all enriching experiences overall, aiding further development and becoming proficient painters over time! In your downtime, read an art book, then set it aside and start your painting session with the objective of putting what you learned into action.

Example Routine: Painting

Establishing a structured routine can be one of the most effective strategies. This chapter presents an example routine that breaks down an efficient 45-minute painting session into three segments. By adhering to this structure, you can cultivate consistency in your practice while ensuring that each session is productive and focused on growth. **Warming Up (5 Minutes)** The first segment of your routine focuses on warming up. Just as athletes engage in stretches and drills to prepare their bodies for competition, artists benefit from similar practices to prepare their minds and hands for creativity. In this warm-up phase, dedicate five minutes to quick sketches, notan studies or color mixing to prepare for the subject. Start by grabbing a sketchbook and a pencil or felt tip marker. Set a five-minute timer and allow yourself to draw anything that comes to mind—simple shapes, objects around you, or even abstract forms. The goal is not perfection but rather to get your hand moving and loosen up your creativity. If you're feeling particularly inspired, try drawing from life; perhaps a plant on your desk or a mug within reach could serve as an interesting subject. If you have a subject in mind for your painting session, then focus on thumbnail-sized sketches to compose that subject. Consider landscape format, portrait, or square options too. Alternatively, if you prefer focusing on color at this stage, use this time to mix color swatches. Choose two or three colors from your subject and try mixing them to prepare for the main session on the canvas. Consider whether the colors are warm or cool and the color's relative darkness or lightness. Are they in shadow (dark) or direct light (light values). This practice will enhance your understanding of color theory and confidence in using paint. This initial segment sets the tone for the remainder of your session by engaging mind and body in the artistic process—a vital step before diving into more intensive work. Main Painting Exercises (30 Minutes) Once you've warmed up sufficiently, it's time to transition into the core focus of the painting session: dedicated thirty-minute painting exercises. In these moments, concentrate intensely on specific elements such as composition, light effects, texture application, or any area where you seek improvement. Before starting this segment, it's helpful to have a clear idea of what you want to achieve during these thirty minutes—whether it's working on an ongoing project or experimenting with new techniques you've read about previously. If you're continuing with an existing artwork, take stock: what aspects need attention? Are there details requiring refinement? Or would it be beneficial simply to lay down more paint? Use the timer feature on your phone or watch once again; setting strict time limits encourages focus while also fostering productivity under slight pressure—an effective way many artists find success when working against deadlines. As you paint during these thirty minutes: - Pay close attention to brush strokes; consider experimenting with different techniques. - Observe contrasts between light and dark values. - Observe what happens when you warm up or cool down a color relative to the other colors.

Engaging thoughtfully with each brushstroke during this period without distractions allows significant progress toward mastering new skills while minimizing the overwhelm associated with longer projects. Reflection (10 Minutes) After thirty focused minutes have passed quickly yet productively through intense work sessions filled with exploration, comes reflection—the final piece bringing clarity amidst creation's chaos! Use these last ten minutes wisely so that you can assess not only what went well but also where areas remain ripe for growth moving forward. With paper handy—or even just mental notes—evaluate key aspects: - What did you enjoy about today? - Which techniques felt natural? - Where did challenges arise?

Take stock, especially regarding any breakthroughs made today—it's crucially important to partake joyfully in artistic endeavors! Additionally, consider jotting down thoughts indicating which areas might require future exploration based upon outcomes experienced today, thus providing direction towards the next sessions! Reflection solidifies learning gained throughout creative endeavors, ultimately helping ensure improvements show over time through consistent practices undertaken day after day! The Importance of Routine Adopting such routines fosters discipline while cultivating patience—essential components required alongside creativity itself! As daily commitments grow larger, competing interests may threaten precious art-making times, yet adhering steadfastly to established schedules offers respite amid busy lives, affirming dedication to personal artistic journeys! Remember, improvisation has its place too—should inspiration strike mid-session, embrace spontaneity, allowing instincts to guide where needed without fear of straying off course—but maintaining structured segments reinforces consistency, granting clearer paths and unveiling growth over extended periods leading toward ultimate success!

Painting Process Example:

Vibrant Sunset in Acrylics

Of all landscape subjects, sunsets must be one of the most popular. Who can resist the glorious colors across the sky? However, this subject also presents a challenge. The colors are elusive, and the surrounding landscape elements are often dark or in the shade. What do you do with them?

The key is to use a scene as inspiration. I am not trying to copy the scene exactly, as a small-format painting does need a bit more punch. Acrylics are suited to vibrant colors, and I will use this quality to create an eye-catching painting.

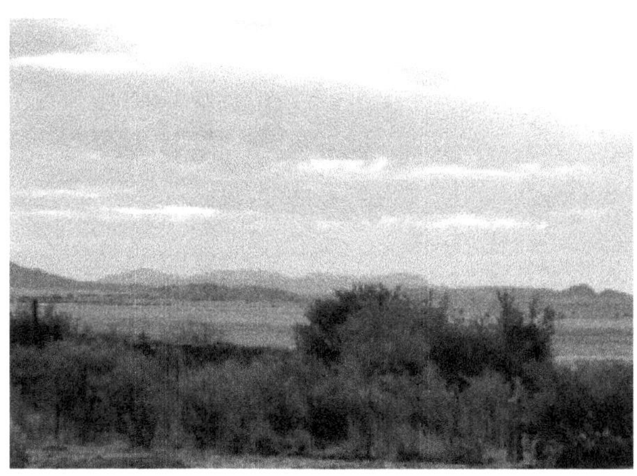

The reference

Materials

I am using a selection of Amsterdam acrylics by Royal Talens and long flat brushes in sizes 8 and 10. The colors are titanium white, Ultramarine blue, Brilliant blue, Naphtol red, magenta, Azo yellow medium, burnt sienna, and yellow ochre.

Composition

The first step is to mark out a horizon line. Avoid dividing the painting in half. As this scene is a sunset, I have lowered the horizon line. A good tip is to roughly sketch the scene in a small thumbnail sketch. Just mark out the big shapes. Then, move on to the painting itself with a plan in place.

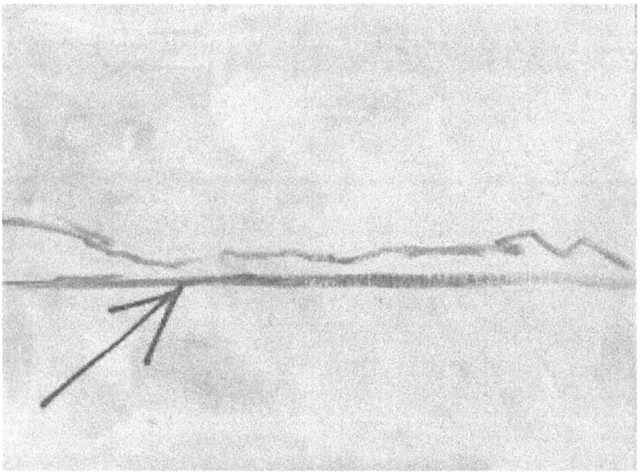

Mark the horizon line

Light and Dark Shapes

Typically, I will add my darkest shapes and my lightest shapes from the start. This gives me my range of values—like a key that opens up the range of colours I will use. Remember that it is the darks that make the lights stand out. Therefore, have a strong dark mass shape that will accentuate your light sunset colors.

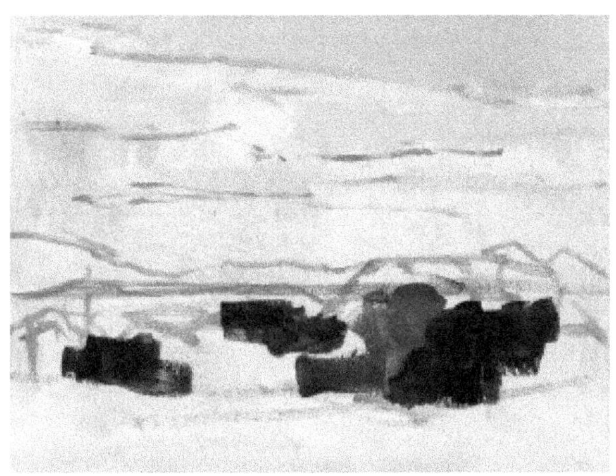

Extreme light an dark shapes first

Important Tip: Use big brushes. Especially when laying the big mass shapes. I am using a number 10 long flat on a panel measuring 26cm x 36cm. Small brushes will result in fiddling and lead to an overworked and fussy painting.

Block in the Mid-Value Mass Shapes

When looking at your scene, try to squint slightly to see simple shapes. These shapes, free from details, are what you are placing on your canvas.

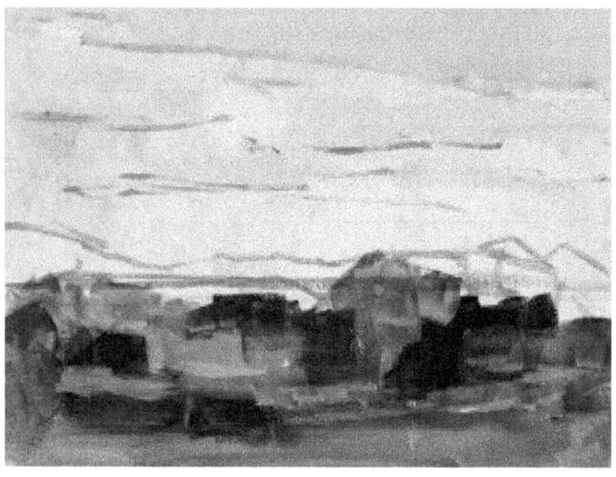

Mid-value shapes

Aerial Perspective

Note the bigger shapes in the foreground with stronger edges and darks. Try to create a sense of distance with receding shapes and softer colors in the distance. Sunset light does tend to warm the entire scene up which makes the space seem less pronounced. But you will need to ensure your colors are cooler in the distance. Add a touch of white and blue where necessary to lighten and cool down the colors.

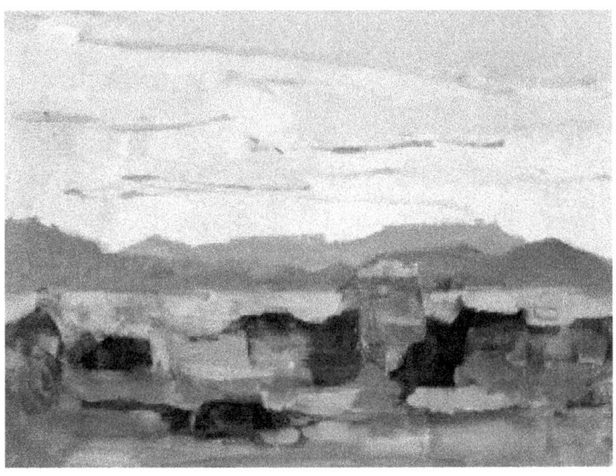

Aerial Perspective colors

Sky Elements

Now, I start blocking in the sky. A sunset is not simply a mass of orange color. You will note that the top of the sky is very light. This is usually overexposed by the camera in relation to the darker colors below. So keep a light sky color at the top but also keep it colorful. I use white, brilliant blue, and a touch of yellow ochre. You can expect some warmth to reflect into this portion, hence the yellow ochre.

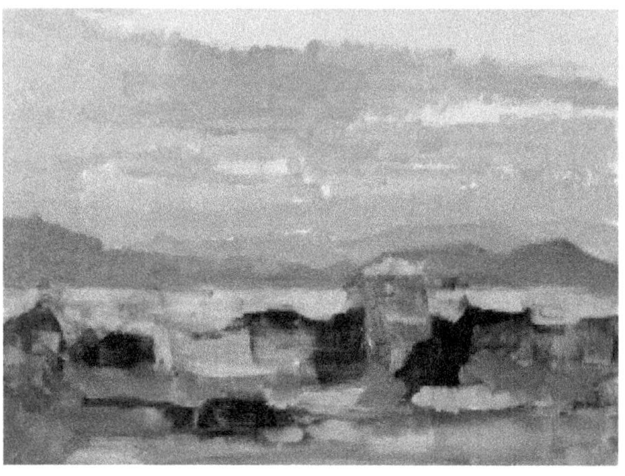

Start adding the sky elements

Foreground

Now, back into the foreground. I can bring that part of the painting forward by darkening the foreground masses. Note that I am not adding white paint. I am just using ultramarine blue, burnt sienna, and orange, with touches of deep purple, too. If you add white too early, your colours will lose intensity and the value contrast that you want.

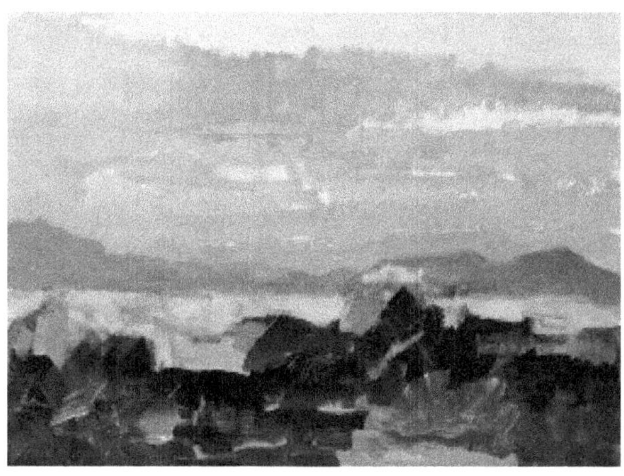

Work the foreground

Add a focal point in the Sky

There are different ways to add a focal point. It can be a high-value contrast or strong, saturated color. But I have chosen to show a glimpse of the setting sun. If you note what is happening in the scene, you can work in added elements from memory, too. In this case, I wanted to show the sun from moments before I took the photo.

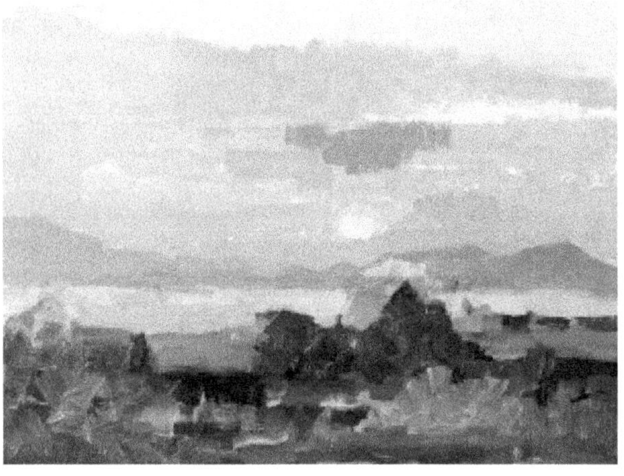

Focal point added on right lower rule of thirds

Start to Adjust Values and Colour Relationships

A sunset gains vibrancy with value contrast and color relationships, just like any other painting. Although the sky above shows strong color, the values are very similar. By bringing in strong value contrast in the dark purple clouds, I can get more vibrancy in the yellow and pink colors. The other key element is color relationships. In this case complementary colours like blue and orange together with yellows and violets. These classic combinations work great. But you can also throw in little sparks of color such as turquoise against the pinkish color too.

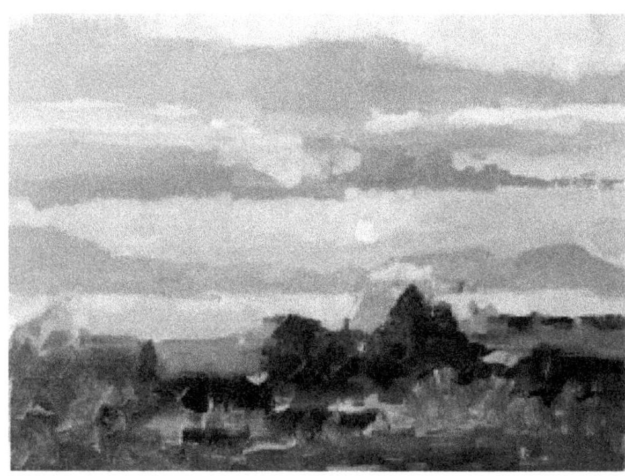

Adjust color and values

The Glowing Effects of Light

Because I have added in the sun above the mountain I need to soften the edges and add some warmth to objects near the sun. This is the natural halo effect that diffuses into the colours nearby.

I also add a few sky colours into the foreground for harmony, but be careful that the values are not too contrasting. I tend to experiment here and will quickly remove anything that stands out too much.

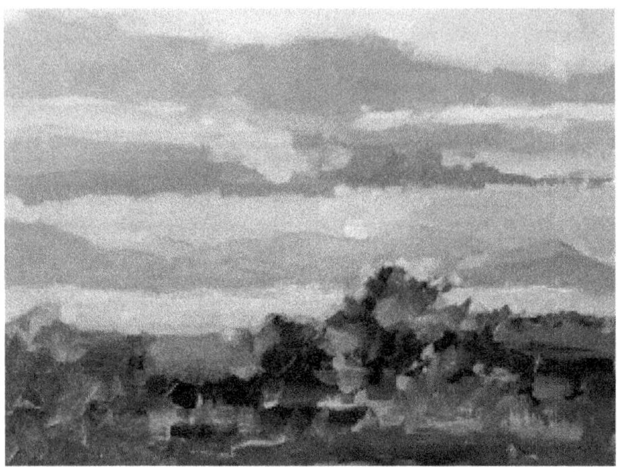

Glowing effects

Make Final Adjustments

This process involves as much personal taste as formal painting technique. I stand back a lot to assess the painting. Perhaps I will take a tea break and then come back to look at the painting with fresh eyes. I have added more colour to the mountains, sparks of colour to the foreground and sky, and a vertical element to the fence posts to balance the horizontals.

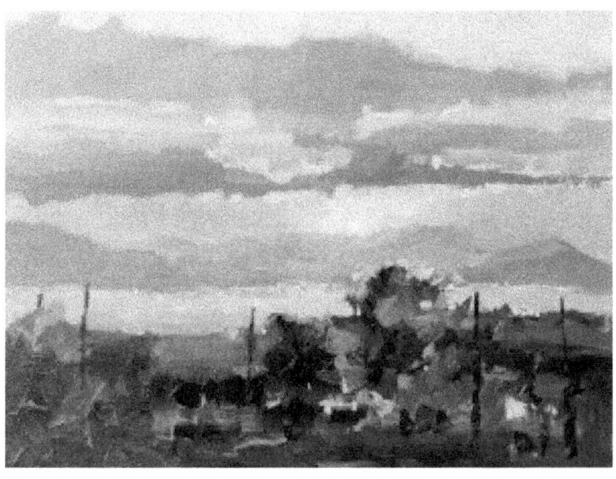

Add final details

An Alternative Ending

The above painting could be the final one. Except like any good superhero movie I decided to add an alternative ending. The painting below has a more subdued foreground with cooler colours. You can decide which version you prefer. Which is another part of sunset paintings that I like: your personal expression is vital. If you want a soft and gentle painting then use less saturated colours and softer edges. If you want punchy colour and vibrancy, like this one, then do not hold back.

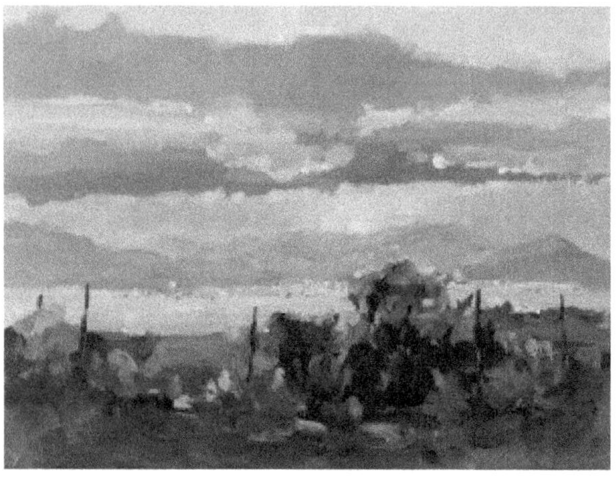

Alternative ending: note foreground

Conclusion

You must have fun with your forty-five-minute-a-day paintings. For example, with this sunset, throw in an unexpected spark of color. See how that adds energy to the scene. Avoid the typical silhouette against an orange sky. Instead, look into shadows with cool purples and dark blues. Then, add the punch in the sky with light and dark shapes and interesting color relationships.

Embracing the 6x8" Canvas

For many artists, larger canvases represent grand ideas and ambitious projects. However, smaller formats, particularly the 6x8-inch canvas, have undeniable charm and practicality. This compact size can be a game-changer for those pressed for time or overwhelmed by larger canvasses. The allure of the smaller canvas lies in its accessibility.With just forty-five minutes to spare before your next commitment—a precious window of time that could easily slip away in the hustle of life. In such moments, reaching for a 6x8" canvas or panel allows you to dive into creativity without the daunting prospect of starting a large piece. The small format encourages spontaneity and experimentation, enabling you to try new techniques or styles without feeling burdened by expectations. One of the greatest benefits of working on smaller canvases is that they allow for rapid skill development. The more frequently you paint, the faster your growth will be as an artist. By focusing on miniatures like the 6x8", you can produce numerous pieces within a short timeframe, each serving as both practice and exploration. This consistent output enriches your portfolio and builds your confidence as you witness firsthand improvements in your technique. Think about this, too. The small panel does not mean small subjects. You can capture vast landscapes in a small panel like this. It comes down to simplifying a scene into the essential shapes, values, and colors. If you can do this, you are truly seen as an artist. Also, the small canvas does not mean little brushstrokes. The large paint-filled stroke provides the biggest reward. You get a generous, juicy, gem-like stroke of paint that is a delight for the artist and viewer.

Due to their limited space, smaller paintings force us to make decisive choices about composition and color usage. Each brushstroke must count; every detail becomes deliberate rather than incidental. This focus on precision fosters greater attention to elements like light, shadow, texture, and form—all essential components that contribute significantly to overall impact. As you explore this new dimension offered by a 6x8" canvas, consider how it presents unique opportunities for expressive work and creative risk-taking that might feel intimidating on bigger surfaces. For example, working within such constraints allows room for bold abstract brushwork—the glow of sunset reflected upon water, for example—described in one or two big strokes where the paint volume describes everything simply yet decisively. In addition to enhancing skill development and encouraging creative risk-taking while maintaining simplicity regarding materials used (a few brushes plus basic colors suffice), embracing small formats also promotes regular practice habits crucial for long-term growth as an artist—especially if time feels scarce during busy periods! Set aside just thirty minutes each day dedicated solely to creating miniature masterpieces. Follow the routine suggested in the previous chapter. This routine will foster consistency and cultivate joy amidst productivity! After weeks of nurturing, every completed piece will be added to your collection, making these tiny wonders tangible evidence of progress! As days turn into weeks filled with exciting discoveries made along this journey, exploring different themes/colors/ techniques over multiple sessions fueled purely by enthusiasm rather than obligation ultimately leads to discovering one's true artistic voice amidst challenges faced along the way! Consider establishing personal challenges around completing specific numbers within set timelines—for example, aiming at finishing five paintings weekly using distinct palettes/styles/motifs! Tracking progress visually through photographs taken throughout stages gives further motivation while simultaneously fostering accountability, ensuring commitment stays strong even when life gets hectic outside studio doors. Also, remember: art isn't merely about producing finished products—it's inherently intertwined, deeply rooted experiences gathered throughout the process itself, leading toward genuine connections formed between creators/viewers alike, allowing intimate exchanges to flourish beyond the confines of limited physical boundaries encompassed under a single frame surrounding singular creation!

Creating a Large Body of Work

One of the most gratifying experiences is witnessing the tangible accumulation of your art. As you dedicate time to honing your craft, especially in manageable segments like 45 minutes each day, you will find that these small efforts can lead to substantial results. The process enriches your skills and allows you to build a comprehensive collection that could form the core of an exhibition, grow your sales, or simply become a testament to your artistic growth. The act of creating art is inherently rewarding. Still, there's an additional layer of satisfaction when you observe the physical manifestation of your creativity—your paintings lined up on a wall or stacked neatly in a portfolio. This collection serves as more than just artwork; it acts as an archive that tells the story of where you began and how far you've come. Each piece reflects not only technical skills but also emotional journeys and personal explorations. As artists, we often focus on individual pieces without considering how they contribute to our overall body of work. However, understanding this broader perspective can be transformative. When you take time each day to paint—even if it's just for 45 minutes—you are setting yourself up for success in ways beyond immediate artistic expression. You're cultivating a large body of work that can serve multiple purposes down the line. Imagine entering an exhibition showcasing a year's worth of paintings created during those daily sessions. The diverse styles and themes represented not only highlight your versatility but also create discussions around continuity and evolution in art—something galleries actively seek when curating shows or selecting featured artists for representation. Building this catalog begins with intention; it requires a commitment to producing work regularly while remaining open to experimentation. Allowing yourself space for exploration will naturally lead to finding unique voices within your creations. One significant advantage comes from having such diversity within a body of work: potential clients are drawn toward artists who showcase both consistency and variety in their portfolios. This balance can position you favorably within competitive markets where galleries look for fresh yet cohesive representations from their artists. Having numerous pieces at hand means that when opportunities arise—be it exhibitions or sales—you are equipped with options ready for presentation instead of scrambling last minute trying to create something new under pressure. Creating a large body doesn't mean cranking out paintings at breakneck speed; rather, it involves nurturing ideas over time while allowing them room to breathe before finalizing them into finished pieces worthy enough for display or sale. One effective way to ensure continuous output is through thematic series—a set group connected by subject matter or style helps streamline creative thought processes and final presentations, further strengthening collections aimed at future exhibitions or clientele pursuits. Consider the series of 6x8 paintings by renowned artist Kevin Macpherson called "Reflections on a Pond". This series of paintings captures 365 days of the same scene. An amazing achievement and a record of stunning light effects on the same scene. Consider starting a similar project centered around specific themes such as seasons changing throughout nature, like winter landscapes transitioning into vibrant spring blooms; capturing moments witnessed during travels abroad reflected upon canvases depicting local architecture found along winding streets rich with culture; exploring emotions tied closely around human experiences through abstract expressions reflecting joy versus sorrow portrayed visually using color palettes contrasting light against the darkness—the possibilities are endless! Another critical aspect is consistency—not merely regarding frequency but quality, too! Establishing routines helps foster discipline where inspiration may sometimes wane due to its cyclical nature influenced by external factors outside control (such as weather changes affecting moods). In this instance, the discipline of the process will carry you through these ups and downs. Ultimately, remember that accumulating a body of artwork goes beyond mere statistics; instead, it serves a higher purpose, enabling connections between collector and artist. Forge ahead and who knows where the journey will lead you. You can be sure however that it will be a rewarding journey and therefore worth the effort.

Approaching Diverse Subjects Quickly

As artists, we often gravitate toward familiar themes and subjects. These comfort zones can provide a sense of security but also stifle creativity and limit our growth. In this chapter, we will explore the benefits of approaching diverse subjects quickly and how dedicating just 45 minutes a day to this practice can dramatically enhance your artistic repertoire. As already discussed, using small canvases allows you to find enough time to paint. This flexibility allows you to explore landscapes, still lives, portraits, and abstract compositions, all within a short timeframe. This diversity of subject matter within a reasonable timeframe will expand your horizons and build confidence. Imagine setting up your easel in a sunlit corner of your home or studio with a small canvas before you. You have only 45 minutes; what will you choose to create? Perhaps today's inspiration is drawn from the vibrant flowers blooming in your garden or the interesting shadows cast by objects on your desk. This limited time constraint encourages quick decision-making and spontaneity—two elements that are vital for nurturing creativity. When engaging with diverse subjects, it's important not to overthink your choices. Allow yourself to paint what calls out to you at that moment rather than striving for an idealistic vision or preconceived notion of what should be created. This approach fosters an environment where exploration reigns supreme; each piece becomes an opportunity for discovery rather than a pressure-laden task. As you begin experimenting with different subjects regularly, you'll notice significant growth in technique and confidence. Each new painting becomes another chance to test your skills and challenge yourself creatively. For instance, if you've primarily painted landscapes but decide one day to tackle portraiture instead, you'll be stepping outside of your comfort zone—a move that can lead to unexpected breakthroughs. Over time this practice builds resilience; even if some pieces do not turn out as expected—or perhaps especially because they don't—you learn valuable lessons about how different elements interact through trial-and-error experiences. This newfound confidence tends not only toward technical skill improvement but also emotional depth within artistic expression in itself—allowing freer flows from imagination into tangible form without being hindered by fear or self-doubt regarding 'success' versus 'failure.' Inspiration starts flowing more naturally—ideas spark quickly while developing a greater willingness to take risks creatively, which becomes second nature over time! If you incorporate these experiments and results in your daily journal you will develop a deeper appreciation of your artistic development. Does this all seem too much? It is easier than you may think as you are not committing a lot of time. Forty-five minutes painting. Less than five minutes journaling your progress. Give it a go.

Finding Inspiration in Daily Life

Finding inspiration in everyday life is one of the most valuable skills you can develop as an artist. While grand landscapes and carefully arranged still lives have their place, often, it's the simple, unassuming moments that spark creativity. This chapter will help you shift your perspective to see beauty and potential in the mundane.

The Hunt for New Subjects: Every completed painting boosts your confidence and curiosity. As you paint more, you train your eye to notice details that may have gone unnoticed. A finished canvas opens the door to fresh ideas, and suddenly, potential subjects appear everywhere—in your home, in nature, in urban settings, or even in ordinary objects.

Look around: What catches your eye? Perhaps it's the way sunlight filters through a window, casting soft shadows on a wall, or the steam rising from a cup of coffee on a chilly morning. Maybe it's an old chair with peeling paint or vibrant flowers growing from cracks in the sidewalk. These scenes hold stories waiting to be told through your art.

To cultivate this habit, set aside time each day for observation. Take walks without a specific destination, and allow yourself to wander and absorb your surroundings. Carry a sketchbook with you—quick sketches can remind you of scenes that struck you as noteworthy.

As an artist, remember that every observation matters. It's not always about painting elaborate compositions but capturing those fleeting moments that resonate with emotion or provoke thought.

Capturing Moments Quickly: Once you've trained yourself to discover new subjects, the next step is capturing them quickly before they fade. Small paintings are perfect for this, as they force clarity and efficiency in composition and technique.

Consider plein air painting or working from life, where time constraints may limit your observation time. The goal isn't to achieve photo-realism but to capture the essence of a scene—its atmosphere, color, and texture.

When working on small canvases, prioritize simplicity. Focus on essential elements like light and shadow instead of intricate details. Your goal should be to convey emotion through color and movement, using dynamic brushwork to bring your scene to life.

Remember, not every piece needs to be perfect. Embrace imperfections—they add authenticity and spontaneity to your work.

Finding Inspiration Beyond Traditional Sources

To avoid creative stagnation, explore unconventional sources of inspiration. Music, literature, and other art forms can influence your approach to painting. For example, listening to different music genres while you paint can create unique atmospheres and encourage experimentation.

Social media can also be a valuable tool. Connect with fellow artists worldwide, share insights, and build a supportive community that fosters growth.

Creating Your Own Inspiration Rituals

Consider establishing rituals to nurture your creativity. Whether it's a daily walk, listening to music, or simply observing your surroundings, these practices can help you tap into a well of inspiration.

Finding inspiration doesn't require extravagant settings or elaborate concepts. Look closely at the simplicity around you, and you'll discover that beauty exists everywhere if you want to see it.

Setting Realistic Goals and Milestones

Setting realistic goals is crucial for artistic growth. Whether you're a beginner exploring your creativity or an experienced artist refining your skills, clear objectives provide direction and motivation. This chapter explores the importance of short-term and long-term goals, how they connect, and strategies for incorporating them into your daily practice.

Short-Term Goals: Building Momentum

Short-term goals are like stepping stones in your artistic journey. These achievable objectives can be completed quickly, offering immediate satisfaction and a sense of accomplishment. For example, you might aim to complete one small painting every two days. The forty-five-minute concept does not mean a new painting every day. It is about using forty-five minutes a day to further your artistic journey, career or whatever you want to call it. This goal is specific enough to keep you focused but flexible enough to fit into your schedule. Alternatively, you could set a monthly target of four or five paintings, allowing for more substantial works while maintaining momentum.

Short-term goals break down larger aspirations into manageable tasks, helping you stay motivated and build confidence with each completed piece. Tracking your progress is also essential—it serves as a record of your journey and a reminder of how far you've come. Once again, consider keeping an art journal to document completed pieces and the insights you gain along the way. Celebrating these small victories reinforces positive habits and highlights areas for improvement.

Long-Term Goals: Defining Your Vision

While short-term goals provide structure, they must align with a broader long-term vision for your art. This overarching perspective gives your efforts purpose and ensures that even disciplined work doesn't feel aimless over time. Reflect on where you want to be as an artist in five or ten years. Do you dream of exhibiting in galleries, selling work online, or mastering a specific style? Maybe get the basics of painting before taking art workshops locally. For instance, how about traveling abroad to take a workshop once a year in Tuscany? Your dreams can come true with focus and planning.

Clarity about your long-term vision acts as a guiding beacon. It gives meaning to each brushstroke, transforming your daily practice into part of a larger, significant journey. To make this vision actionable, develop key milestones, such as participating in local exhibitions within six months or creating an online portfolio within three months. These milestones propel you toward achieving your dreams over time.

Another important consideration for the older artist is fulfilling a creative purpose in life. Perhaps you have neglected this significant need but now is your opportunity. I know how important this is, so do not hesitate another day. Put your goals into writing and begin your painting journey now.

Flexibility and Adaptation

It's important to remain flexible as life may bring unexpected challenges that require adjustments. However, these changes shouldn't derail your journey. Instead, see them as opportunities to refine your goals and adapt your approach while focusing on your broader aspirations.

Setting goals might seem daunting, especially when faced with endless possibilities. But remember, goal-setting comes from a sincere passion, leading to genuine expression on the canvas. It's vital to articulate your ambitions and follow through with your artistic endeavors.

Embracing the Journey

In summary, find a balance between ambition and the need to appreciate the nuances of your journey. By marrying short-term accomplishments with long-term visions, you ensure that your artistry blossoms fully, becoming a fulfilling expression of your creative self.

As you embark on this adventure, guided by realistic goals, remember that every moment spent refining your techniques will yield rewards. Art's journey is beautiful, filled with endless potential and vibrant discoveries. Embrace it with enthusiasm, and let your artistry flourish.

Set Your True North and Keep Going

As you embark on the painting journey, remember that the process is as important as the final product. True growth comes not just from the finished work but from every brushstroke, every struggle, and every moment of reflection.

Take time to look back at your progress. Reflect on your earlier works. Notice how your skills have improved, your color choices have evolved, and your confidence has grown. These reflections remind you of your progress and the value of your dedication.

Keep a journal for your artistic journey. Document your thoughts, challenges, and breakthroughs. This practice fosters mindfulness, allowing you to engage more deeply with your work. Every few weeks, compare your past and present pieces. This visual comparison will highlight your growth and the new directions your art has taken.

Daily practice is key to improvement. Just 45 minutes a day can make a difference. Approach this routine with curiosity and excitement, not as a chore but as an opportunity to explore and grow. The goal isn't perfection but discovery and expression.

Mistakes are part of the learning process. When things don't go as planned, view these moments as opportunities for growth, not failure. Experiment with different techniques, styles, and mediums. Play with your art. Each experiment brings you closer to finding your unique voice.

Seek inspiration beyond the usual sources. Explore nature, visit galleries, or join workshops. Engaging with other artists and different environments can spark new ideas and perspectives.

Above all, embrace change and progress. Art evolves, just like life. There will be highs and lows, but each moment contributes to your artistic development. Be patient with yourself, honor your progress, and cherish the journey.

Every brushstroke tells a story, reflecting your emotions and experiences. Continue to paint passionately, knowing that this journey will lead you closer to discovering the true essence of your artistry.

Onwards!

About the Author

I want to thank you personally for reading this book. If you have reached this far, you are in the "one percent" category of people who finish what they started. Maybe we can shift that statistic a bit higher? Thanks to your self-discipline, you have achieved much. You will enjoy your life as a creatively awakened individual.

I also want to thank all those artists who study their craft with me. Whether you are a member of my Artist's Live Channel[1], own a course, or watch my YouTube videos[2]. You are also self-disciplined and no doubt experiencing growth in your art. My best wishes to you!

Further learning:

My courses on painting fundamentals: Learn to Paint with Impact[3].

Now, then, back into the third-person:

Author: Malcolm Dewey is a South African artist and writer. He paints in a contemporary Impressionist style and mostly paints landscapes and figures. He teaches painting in various mediums, including oils, acrylics, gouache, watercolor, and pastels. Malcolm sells his works to collectors all over the world, and his gallery can be viewed at www.malcolmdeweyfineart.com[4]

---

1. https://malcolmdeweyfineart.newzenler.com/courses/artists-live-membership

2. https://www.youtube.com/MalcolmDewey

3. https://www.malcolmdeweyfineart.com/painting-course.html

Connect with Malcolm on his website to join one of his free tutorials. Also Youtube/MalcolmDewey[5]

Finally, if you enjoyed this book, please give it a review on Amazon. Thank you!

---

4. https://www.malcolmdeweyfineart.com/painting-secrets.html

5. https://www.youtube.com/MalcolmDewey

Also by Malcolm Dewey

An Artist's Guide to Plein Air Painting
How to Loosen Up Your Painting
An Artist's Survival Guide
The Creative Living Book Bundle
The Art of Content Marketing
52 Weeks of Creative Living: Inspiration for Your Creative Soul
Your Artist's Voice
52 Weeks of Creative Mastery
Sell Your Art or Not?
The Creative Awakening
45 Minutes to Mastery

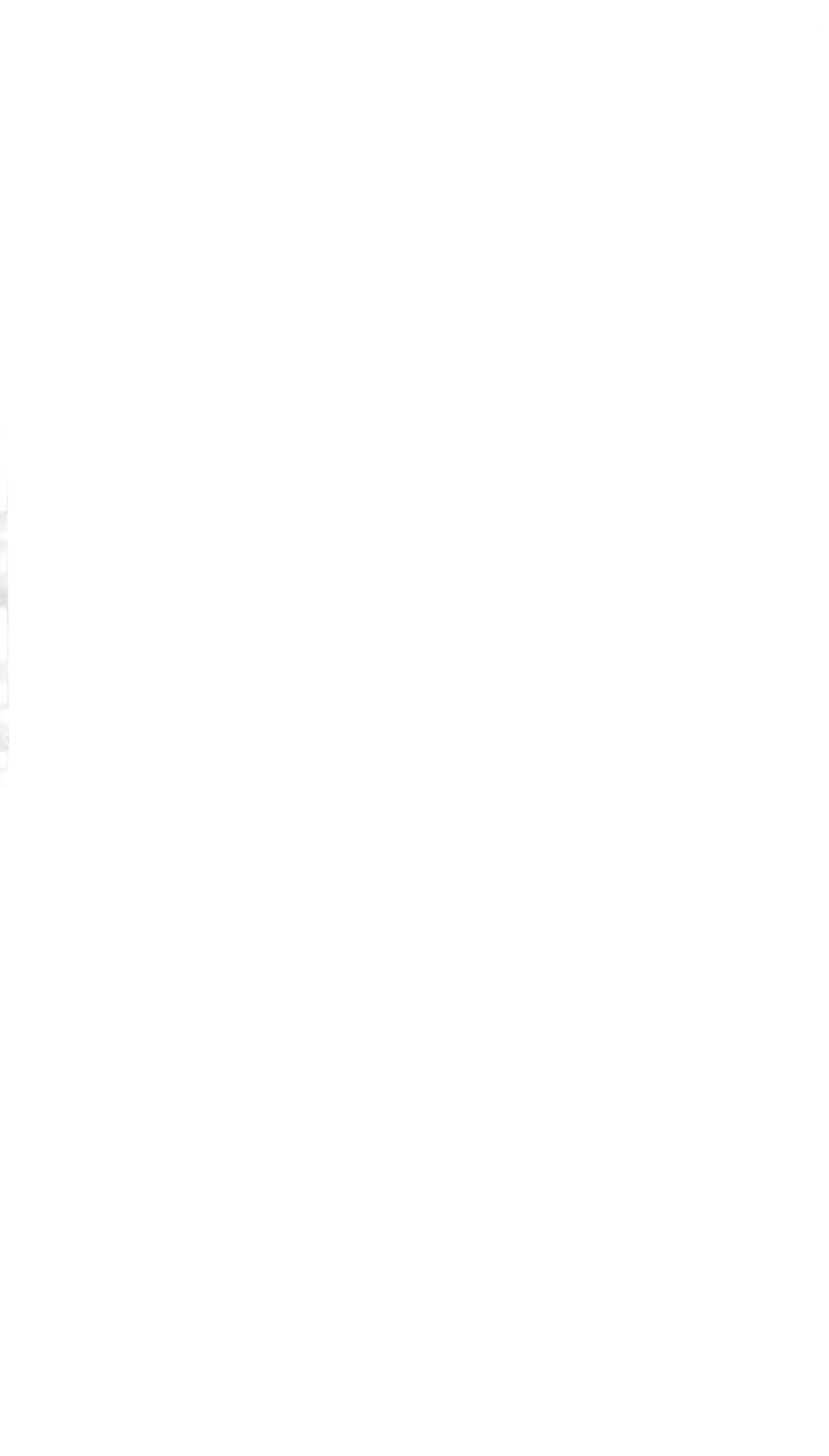